Little People, **BIG DREAMS**™

ERNEST SHACKLETON

Written by
Maria Isabel Sánchez Vegara

Illustrated by
Olivia Holden

Frances Lincoln
Children's Books

Little Ernest was an Irish boy, born on a farm surrounded by rolling green hills. His family had lived in the same county for more than 150 years, and Ernest dreamt of traveling far... further than anyone had ever gone before.

He was six years old when he dug a hole in the back yard, determined to arrive on the other side of the world. Ernest had the four qualities of a good explorer: optimism, patience, idealism, and courage!

Aged 16, Ernest joined the merchant navy and put his heart and soul into becoming a master mariner. He took part in two expeditions trying to reach the South Pole, the southernmost place on Earth.

When Roald Amundsen, a Norwegian explorer, reached it first, Ernest decided to plan a new feat: to cross Antarctica from sea to sea, via the pole. It would be the greatest journey ever attempted!

He placed an advertisement in a newspaper that read:

Men Wanted

*For hazardous journey,
small wages, bitter cold,
long months of complete
darkness, constant danger,
safe return doubtful,
honor and recognition
in case of success.*

Ernest Shackleton

Many qualified men applied for the job. But for Ernest, their ability to work as a team was much more important than experience.

In August 1914, a team of 28 men, 69 sled dogs, several pigs, and a cat named Mrs Chippy headed to Antarctica on a ship called the *Endurance*. It was the most enthusiastic and optimistic crew ever seen!

For months, Ernest and his crew crossed the ocean, greeting the whales and the penguins as they sailed near majestic icebergs. But, one day, their ship became trapped in the ice, unable to move in any direction.

Hoping that when spring came the ship would be released, Ernest decided to stay calm. He used every trick he could think of to cheer his men up and keep them busy, organizing dog races, telling stories, and playing soccer on ice.

Nine long months passed, and the ice started breaking the ship into pieces. Ernest and his men were left on a drifting floe with few supplies left. Their only chance was to drag the lifeboats to open sea in an attempt to reach land.

It took seven days on deep, dark waters for the exhausted crew to reach Elephant Island. Ernest always stood tall at the tiller, keeping morale high. But there was little hope of being rescued in such a vast, uninhabited land.

In an attempt to be rescued, Ernest and five of his men left the crew and set off again on a dangerous journey, looking for the nearest whaling station. Sailors couldn't believe their eyes the day that Ernest walked in, asking for help!

With help at hand, Ernest went back to the island and saved the rest of the crew. Everybody thought it was a miracle that they had all survived, but Ernest never lost faith in bringing his men home.

Little Ernest lived through one of the most incredible adventures of all time. Today, his story inspires an endless crew of dreamers who know that optimism is the truest and most powerful form of courage.

ERNEST SHACKLETON

(Born 1874 • Died 1922)

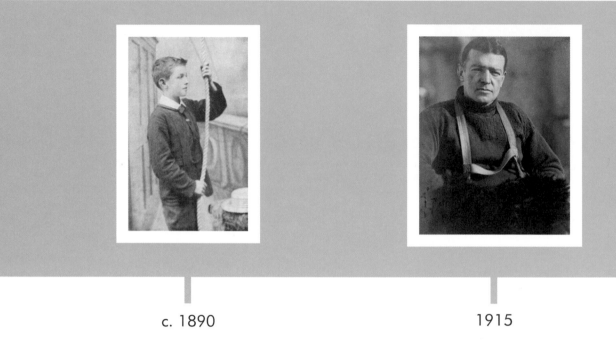

c. 1890

1915

Ernest Henry Shackleton was born on February 15, 1874 in the Irish county of Kildare. The second of ten children, the family moved to London when Shackleton was ten years old. His father Henry, a family doctor, hoped that Ernest would follow in his footsteps into medicine, sending Ernest to be educated at the prestigious Dulwich College. But Ernest had other ideas, and with a desire to explore the world, he joined the merchant navy aged 16. In 1901, he journeyed on his first expedition to Antarctica aboard the *Discovery*. The trip took Shackleton closer to the South Pole than anyone before—and it also forced him home when he got seriously sick. But when Norwegian explorer Roald Amundsen reached the South Pole in 1911, Shackleton knew his expedition days were far from finished. Attempting

1915

1917

to cross Antarctica via the South Pole, Shackleton set out with his crew from London aboard the *Endurance* on August 1, 1914. By early 1915, the ship became trapped in ice, and his crew were forced to live on the floating ice. A year later, they set off in three small boats, reaching dry land on Elephant Island. Taking five of his crew members with him, Shackleton set off in search of help, crossing 800 miles of ocean to reach South Georgia, where they found help at a whaling station. The rest of his crew were rescued 3 months later, all of them surviving to tell the tale. "Difficulties are just things to overcome, after all," Shackleton once remarked. His optimism and perseverance continue to make his Antarctic expeditions some of the greatest adventure stories still told today.

Want to find out more about **Ernest Shackleton?**

Have a read of these great books:

Shackleton's Journey by William Grill

Who Was Ernest Shackleton? by James Buckley

Brimming with creative inspiration, how-to projects, and useful information to enrich your everyday life, Quarto Knows is a favourite destination for those pursuing their interests and passions. Visit our site and dig deeper with our books into your area of interest: Quarto Creates, Quarto Cooks, Quarto Homes, Quarto Lives, Quarto Drives, Quarto Explores, Quarto Gifts, or Quarto Kids.

Text copyright © 2020 Maria Isabel Sánchez Vegara. Illustrations copyright © 2020 Olivia Holden.

Original concept of the series by Maria Isabel Sánchez Vegara, published by Alba Editorial, s.l.u

Produced under trademark licence from Alba Editorial s.l.u and Beautifool Couple S.L.

First Published in the US in 2020 by Frances Lincoln Children's Books, an imprint of The Quarto Group.

100 Cummings Center, Suite 265D, Beverly, MA 01915, USA.

T +1 978-282-9590 F +1 078-283-2742 **www.QuartoKnows.com**

First Published in Spain in 2020 under the title Pequeño & Grande Ernest Shackleton
by Alba Editorial, s.l.u., Baixada de Sant Miquel, 1, 08002 Barcelona

www.albaeditorial.es

A catalogue record for this book is available from the British Library.

ISBN 978-0-7112-4571-6

eISBN 978-0-7112-6192-1

Set in Futura BT.

Published by Katie Cotton • Designed by Sasha Moxon
Edited by Katy Flint • Production by Caragh McAleenan

Manufactured in Guangdong, China CC112020

3 5 7 9 8 6 4 2

Photographic acknowledgements (pages 28-29, from left to right) 1. Used with permission from the Shackleton family. 2. Ernest H. Shackleton. 1915, Frank Hurley/Scott Polar Research Institute, University of Cambridge/Getty Images 3. Frank Hurley And Ernest Shackleton. 1915, Frank Hurley/Scott Polar Research Institute, University of Cambridge/Getty Images 4. Ernest Shackleton Posing in His Officer Uniform. 1917, George Rinhart/Corbis via Getty Images

Collect the *Little People*, **BIG DREAMS™** series:

FRIDA KAHLO

ISBN: 978-1-84780-783-0

COCO CHANEL

ISBN: 978-1-84780-784-7

MAYA ANGELOU

ISBN: 978-1-84780-889-9

AMELIA EARHART

ISBN: 978-1-84780-888-2

AGATHA CHRISTIE

ISBN: 978-1-84780-960-5

MARIE CURIE

ISBN: 978-1-84780-962-9

ROSA PARKS

ISBN: 978-1-78603-018-4

AUDREY HEPBURN

ISBN: 978-1-78603-053-5

EMMELINE PANKHURST

ISBN: 978-1-78603-020-7

ELLA FITZGERALD

ISBN: 978-1-78603-087-0

ADA LOVELACE

ISBN: 978-1-78603-076-4

JANE AUSTEN

ISBN: 978-1-78603-120-4

GEORGIA O'KEEFFE

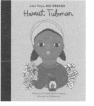
ISBN: 978-1-78603-122-8

HARRIET TUBMAN

ISBN: 978-1-78603-227-0

ANNE FRANK

ISBN: 978-1-78603-229-4

MOTHER TERESA

ISBN: 978-1-78603-230-0

JOSEPHINE BAKER

ISBN: 978-1-78603-228-7

L. M. MONTGOMERY

ISBN: 978-1-78603-233-1

JANE GOODALL

ISBN: 978-1-78603-231-7

SIMONE DE BEAUVOIR

ISBN: 978-1-78603-232-4

MUHAMMAD ALI

ISBN: 978-1-78603-331-4

STEPHEN HAWKING

ISBN: 978-1-78603-333-8

MARIA MONTESSORI

ISBN: 978-1-78603-755-8

VIVIENNE WESTWOOD

ISBN: 978-1-78603-757-2

MAHATMA GANDHI

ISBN: 978-1-78603-787-9

DAVID BOWIE

ISBN: 978-1-78603-332-1

WILMA RUDOLPH

ISBN: 978-1-78603-751-0

DOLLY PARTON

ISBN: 978-1-78603-760-2

BRUCE LEE

ISBN: 978-1-78603-789-3

RUDOLF NUREYEV

ISBN: 978-1-78603-791-6

ZAHA HADID

ISBN: 978-1-78603-745-9

MARY SHELLEY
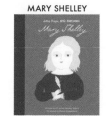
ISBN: 978-1-78603-748-0

MARTIN LUTHER KING JR.

ISBN: 978-0-7112-4567-9

DAVID ATTENBOROUGH
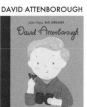
ISBN: 978-0-7112-4564-8

ASTRID LINDGREN

ISBN: 978-0-7112-5217-2

EVONNE GOOLAGONG

ISBN: 978-0-7112-4586-0

BOB DYLAN

ISBN: 978-0-7112-4675-1

ALAN TURING

ISBN: 978-0-7112-4678-2

BILLIE JEAN KING

ISBN: 978-0-7112-4693-5

GRETA THUNBERG
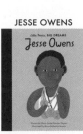
ISBN: 978-0-7112-5645-3

JESSE OWENS

ISBN: 978-0-7112-4583-9

JEAN-MICHEL BASQUIAT

ISBN: 978-0-7112-4580-8

ARETHA FRANKLIN

ISBN: 978-0-7112-4686-7

CORAZON AQUINO

ISBN: 978-0-7112-4684-3

PELÉ

ISBN: 978-0-7112-4573-0

ERNEST SHACKLETON

ISBN: 978-0-7112-4571-6

STEVE JOBS

ISBN: 978-0-7112-4577-8

AYRTON SENNA

ISBN: 978-0-7112-4672-0

LOUISE BOURGEOIS

ISBN: 978-0-7112-4690-4

ELTON JOHN

ISBN: 978-0-7112-5840-2

JOHN LENNON

ISBN: 978-0-7112-5767-2

PRINCE

ISBN: 978-0-7112-5439-8

CHARLES DARWIN

ISBN: 978-0-7112-5771-9

CAPTAIN TOM MOORE
ISBN: 978-0-7112-6209-6

HANS CHRISTIAN ANDERSEN

ISBN: 978-0-7112-5934-8

STEVIE WONDER

ISBN: 978-0-7112-5775-7

MEGAN RAPINOE

ISBN: 978-0-7112-5783-2

MARY ANNING

ISBN: 978-0-7112-5554-8

MALALA YOUSAFZAI

ISBN: 978-0-7112-5904-1

ACTIVITY BOOKS

STICKER ACTIVITY BOOK
ISBN: 978-0-7112-6012-2

COLORING BOOK
ISBN: 978-0-7112-6136-5

LITTLE ME, BIG DREAMS JOURNAL

ISBN: 978-0-7112-4889-2